Zlata Filipović

Zlata

Extracts from Zlata's Diary

With a foreword and afterword by Brian Moses

Zlata with her
diary.

Zlata

Heinemann Educational Publishers
Halley Court, Jordan Hill, Oxford OX2 8EJ
a division of Reed Educational & Professional Publishing Limited

Heinemann is a registered trademark of Reed Educational & Professional
Publishing Limited

OXFORD MELBOURNE AUCKLAND
JOHANNESBURG BLANTYRE GABORONE
IBADAN PORTSMOUTH (NH) USA CHICAGO

© Fixot et les Editions Robert Laffont, Paris, 1993. Published in French under the
title "Le Journal De Zlata", originally published in English by Viking, 1994.
This edition published in 1999.

The moral right of the proprietor has been asserted.

03 02
10 9 8 7 6 5 4 3 2

British Library Cataloguing in Publication Data. A catalogue record for this book is
available from the British Library.

ISBN 0 435 09671 0   "Extracts from Zlata's Diary" single copy
ISBN 0 435 09672 9   "Extracts from Zlata's Diary" 6 copy pack

Photos: Sipa Press/Alexandra Boulat, cover, title page, pages 9, 10, 13, 19, 29. Paul Lowe/Magnum Photos,
pages 3, 6, 16, 24. Martin Mayer/Network, page 5. AFP EPA/A Niedringhaus, page 22. Popperfoto/AFP, page
26. Illustrations: M2, pages 30, 31.

Designed by M2. Printed and bound in the UK

All information and borders on maps of former Yugoslavia are correct at time of going to press.

You might like to learn more about Zlata by reading the full version of her diary.
It is published in the UK by Penguin, ISBN 0-140-37463-9

Introduction

Zlata Filipović was ten years old when, in the autumn of 1991, she began writing a diary. In it she recorded the events in her life. She called her diary 'Mimmy' and treated it like a close friend with whom she could share her thoughts and feelings.

Zlata had a comfortable home with her parents in Sarajevo, the capital city of Bosnia-Herzegovina. Like many schoolgirls, Zlata enjoyed spending time with her friends, her school life, pop music, fashion and food. In Zlata's words her life '... was wonderful. Everyday there is something nice – mountains, skiing, the seaside, friends.'

Then, in 1992, life in Bosnia-Herzegovina changed. A civil war started between the Bosnian Serb people who wanted to stay part of Yugoslavia, and the Bosnian Croats and Muslims who wanted Bosnia-Herzegovina to be an independent country. People who, up until then, had lived and worked together, started fighting each other. Very soon, Zlata was filling her diary with her growing anxieties: 'You can simply feel that something is coming, something very bad.'

When the war came to Sarajevo, Zlata's life changed dramatically. The city was shelled, school closed and Zlata lost contact with her friends. Many nights were spent sheltering in cellars and there was a constant danger of being shot at by snipers. Entries in her diary reported the horrific events that took place in the streets of Sarajevo.

Zlata's diary was written with fear, but also with sorrow and anger for the childhood that was being taken from her. 'War has suddenly entered our town, our thoughts, our lives. It's terrible.'

Brian Moses

Zlata's friends and relations

Below are some of the people mentioned by Zlata in her diary:

Alicia Her mother

Bobar family Close neighbours and family friends: Grandma Mira, Auntie Boda and Uncle Žika, Maja and Bojana (their two daughters)

Braco Her mother's brother

Braco Lajtner Family friend, married to Keka, Martina's and Matea's father

Cicko Her canary

Keka Family friend, married to Braco Lajtner, Martina's and Matea's mother

Malik Her father

Mirna Her best friend

Neda Her mother's best friend from work

Srdjan Her parents' friend

Monday, 2 September 1991

Behind me – a long, hot summer and the happy days of summer holidays; ahead of me – a new school year. I'm starting fifth grade. I'm looking forward to seeing my friends at school, to being together again. Some of them I haven't seen since the day the school bell rang, marking the end of term. I'm glad we'll be together again, and share all the worries and joys of going to school.

 Mirna, Bojana, Marijana, Ivana, Maša, Azra, Minela, Nadža – we're all together again.

Sarajevo in 1991.

Sunday, 6 October 1991

I'm watching the American Top 20 on MTV. I don't remember
a thing, who's in what place.

I feel great because I've just eaten a 'Four Seasons'
PIZZA with ham, cheese, ketchup and mushrooms. It was
yummy. Daddy bought it for me at Galija's (the pizzeria
around the corner). Maybe that's why I didn't remember who
took what place — I was too busy enjoying the pizza.

I've finished studying and tomorrow I can go to school
BRAVELY, without being afraid of getting a bad grade. I
deserve a good grade because I studied all weekend and I
didn't even go out to play with my friends in the park.
The weather is nice and we usually play 'monkey in the
middle', talk and go for walks. Basically, we have fun.

Zlata writing her diary at home in Sarajevo.

Wednesday, 23 October 1991

There's a real war going on in Dubrovnik. It's being badly shelled. People are in shelters, they have no water, no electricity, the phones aren't working. We see horrible pictures on TV. Mummy and Daddy are worried. Is it possible that such a beautiful town is being destroyed? Mummy and Daddy are especially fond of it. It was there, in the Ducal Palace, that they picked up a quill and wrote 'YES' to spending the rest of their lives together. Mummy says it's the most beautiful town in the world and it mustn't be destroyed!!!

We're worried about Srdjan (my parents' best friend who lives and works in Dubrovnik, but his family is still in Sarajevo) and his parents. How are they coping with everything that's happening over there? Are they alive? We're trying to talk to him with the help of a radio ham, but it's not working. Bokica (Srdjan's wife) is miserable. Every attempt to get some news ends in failure. Dubrovnik is cut off from the rest of the world.

Tuesday, 12 November 1991

The situation in Dubrovnik is getting worse
and worse. We managed to learn through the
radio ham that Srdjan is alive and that he
and his parents are all right. The pictures
on TV are awful. People are starving. We're
wondering about how to send a package to
Srdjan. It can be done somehow through
Caritas[1]. Daddy is still going to the
reserves, he comes home tired. When will it
stop? Daddy says maybe next week. Thank God.

1. The Catholic humanitarian aid and relief organization.

Thursday, 14 November 1991

Daddy isn't going to the reserves any more. Hooray!!!...
Now we'll be able to go to Jahorina and Crnotina on
weekends. But, petrol has been a problem lately. Daddy
often spends hours waiting in the queue for petrol, he
goes outside of town to get it, and often comes home
without getting the job done.

 Together with Bokica we sent a package to Srdjan. We
learned through the radio ham that they have nothing to
eat. They have no water, Srdjan swapped a bottle of
whiskey for five litres of water. Eggs, apples, potatoes
- the people of Dubrovnik can only dream about them.

Zlata with her parents, Alicia and Malik.

Monday, 2 December 1991

It's my birthday tomorrow. Mummy is making a cake and all the rest, because we really celebrate in our house. One day is for my friends, that's 3 December, and the next day is for family friends and relatives. Mummy and I are getting a tombola together, and thinking up questions for the children's quiz. This year we have birthday cups, plates and napkins all with little red apples on them. They're sweet. Mummy bought them in Pula. The cake will be shaped like a butterfly and ... this time I'll be blowing out eleven candles. I'll have to take a deep breath and blow them all out at once.

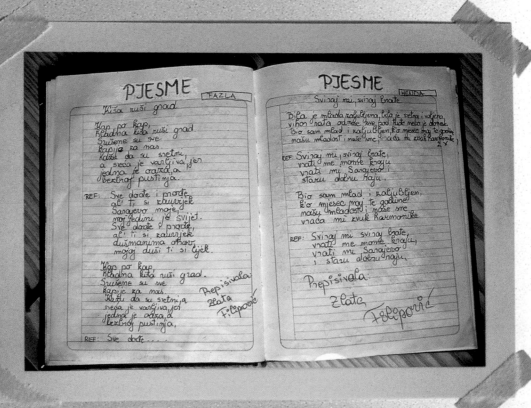

Original pages from Zlata's diary.

Thursday, 19 December 1991

Sarajevo has launched an appeal (on TV)
called 'Sarajevo Helps the Children of
Dubrovnik'. In Srdjan's parcel we put a nice
New Year's present for him to give to some
child in Dubrovnik. We made up a package of
sweets, chocolates, vitamins, a doll, some
books, pencils, notebooks — whatever we
could manage, hoping to bring happiness to
some innocent child who has been stopped by
the war from going to school, playing,
eating what he wants and enjoying his
childhood. It's a nice little package. I
hope it makes whoever gets it happy. That's
the idea. I also wrote a New Year's card
saying I hoped the war in Dubrovnik would
end soon.

Tuesday, 14 January 1992

I yawned, opened my pen and started to write: I'm
listening to the music from "Top Gun" on Good Vibrations
(on the radio). Something else is on now. I've just
destroyed the back page of "Bazar" [a fashion magazine].
I talked to Mummy on the phone. She's at work.
 I have something to tell you. Every night I dream that
I'm asking Michael Jackson for his autograph, but either
he won't give it to me or his secretary writes it, and
then all the letters melt, because Michael Jackson
didn't write them. Sad. Poor me. Ha, ha, ha, ha, I have
to, ha, ha, ha, ha, laugh, ha, ha, ha, ha.

Tuesday, 4 February 1992

School has started. Responsibilities ... I've just come
back from music school. Well, it was OK, I guess.
 I didn't tell you, dear Diary, that I have a notebook
in which I paste fashion pictures. I have photos of
Linda Evangelista, Claudia Schiffer, Cindy Crawford,
Yasmin Le Bon.

Thursday, 5 March 1992

Oh, God! Things are heating up in Sarajevo. On Sunday
(1 March), a small group of armed civilians (as they say
on TV) killed a Serbian wedding guest and wounded the
priest. On 2 March (Monday) the whole city was full of
barricades. There were '1,000' barricades. We didn't
even have bread. At 18.00 people got fed up and went out
into the streets. The procession set out from the
cathedral. It went past the parliament building and made

its way through the entire city. Several people were wounded at the Marshal Tito army barracks. People sang and cried 'Bosnia, Bosnia', 'Sarajevo, Sarajevo', 'We'll live together' and 'Come and join us'. Zdravko Grebo[2] said on the radio that history was in the making.

Zlata behind a barbed wire barricade.

2. President of the Soros Foundation in Sarajevo and editor-in-chief of ZID, the independent radio station.

Friday, 6 March 1992

Things are back to normal.

Monday, 30 March 1992

Hey, Diary! You know what I think? Since Anne Frank
called her diary Kitty, maybe I could give you a name
too. What about:

ASFALTINA   PIDŽAMETA
ŠEFIKA   HIKMETA
ŠEVALA   MIMMY

or something else???
 I'm thinking, thinking...
 I've decided! I'm going to call you
 MIMMY
 All right, then, let's start.

Dear Mimmy,

It's almost half-term. We're all studying for our tests.
Tomorrow we're supposed to go to a classical music
concert at the Skenderija Hall. Our teacher says we
shouldn't go because there will be 10,000 people, pardon
me, children, there, and somebody might take us as
hostages or plant a bomb in the concert hall. Mummy
says I shouldn't go. So I won't.

 Love,
 Zlata

Sunday, 5 April 1992

Dear Mimmy,

I'm trying to concentrate so I can do my homework (reading), but I simply can't. Something is going on in town. You can hear gunfire from the hills. Columns of people are spreading out from Dobrinja. They're trying to stop something, but they themselves don't know what. You can simply feel that something is coming, something very bad. On TV I see people in front of the B-H parliament building. The radio keeps playing the same song: 'Sarajevo, My Love'. That's all very nice, but my stomach is still in knots and I can't concentrate on my homework any more.

Mimmy, I'm afraid of WAR!!!

Zlata

When the electricity in Sarajevo was cut off,
Zlata would write her diary by candlelight.

Monday, 6 April 1992

Dear Mimmy

Yesterday the people in front of the parliament tried
peacefully to cross the Vrbanja bridge. But they were shot
at. Who? How? Why? A girl, a medical student from
Dubrovnik, was KILLED. Her blood spilled onto the bridge.
In her final moments all she said was: 'Is this Sarajevo?'
HORRIBLE, HORRIBLE, HORRIBLE!
 NO ONE AND NOTHING HERE IS NORMAL!

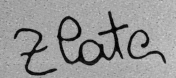

Thursday, 9 April 1992

Dear Mimmy,

I'm not going to school. All the schools in
Sarajevo are closed. There's danger hiding in
these hills above Sarajevo. But I think things
are slowly calming down. The heavy shelling and
explosions have stopped. There's occasional
gunfire, but it quickly falls silent. Mummy and
Daddy aren't going to work. They're buying food
in huge quantities. Just in case, I guess. God
forbid!
   Still, it's very tense. Mummy is beside herself,
Daddy tried to calm her down. Mummy has long
conversations on the phone. She calls, other
people call, the phone is in constant use.

Zlata

Tuesday, 14 April 1992

Dear Mimmy,

People are leaving Sarajevo. The airport, train and bus stations are packed. I saw sad pictures on TV of people parting. Families, friends separating. Some are leaving, others staying. It's so sad. Why? These people and children aren't guilty of anything. Keka and Braco came early this morning. They're in the kitchen with Mummy and Daddy, whispering. Keka and Mummy are crying. I don't think they know what to do — whether to stay or to go. Neither way is good.

Zlata

Saturday, 18 April 1992

Dear Mimmy,

There's shooting, shells are falling. This really is WAR. Mummy and Daddy are worried, they sit up until late at night, talking. They're wondering what to do, but it's hard to know. Whether to leave and split up, or stay here together. Keka wants to take me to Ohrid. Mummy can't make up her mind — she's constantly in tears. She tries to hide it from me, but I see everything. I see that things aren't good here. There's no peace. War has suddenly entered our town, our thoughts, our lives. It's terrible.

It's also terrible that Mummy has packed my suitcase.

Love, Zlata

Zlata and her parents with their cases packed, hoping to leave Sarajevo. They tried to leave several times before they finally succeeded.

Wednesday, 22 April 1992

Dear Mimmy,

We spent the whole night in the Bobars' cellar. We went there around 21.30 and came home at about 10.30 the next morning. I slept from 4.00 to 9.30 a.m. It boomed and shook really badly last night.

Zlata

Sunday, 26 April 1992

Dear Mimmy,

We spent Thursday night with the Bobars again. The next day we had no electricity. We had no bread, so for the first time in her life Mummy baked some. She was scared how it would turn out. It turned out like bread — good bread. That was the day I was supposed to go to Ohrid with M & M [Martina and Matea, Zlata's friends]. But I didn't, and neither did they.

Ciao!

Your
Zlata

Saturday, 2 May 1992

Dear Mimmy,

Today was truly, absolutely the worst day ever in Sarajevo. The shooting started around noon. Mummy and I moved into the hall. Daddy was in his office, under our flat, at the time. We told him on the interphone to run quickly to the downstairs lobby where we'd meet him. We brought Cicko [Zlata's canary] with us. The gunfire was getting worse, and we couldn't get over the wall to the Bobars, so we ran down to our own cellar.

 The cellar is ugly, dark, smelly. Mummy, who's terrified of mice, had two fears to cope with. The three of us were in the same corner as the other day. We listened to the pounding shells, the shooting, the thundering noise overhead. We even heard planes. At one moment I realized that this awful cellar was the only place that could save our lives. Suddenly, it started to look almost warm and nice. It was the only way we could defend ourselves against all this terrible shooting. We heard glass shattering on our street. Horrible. I put my fingers in my ears to block out the terrible sounds.

Ciao!

Zlata

Sunday, 3 May 1992

Dear Mimmy,

Daddy managed to run across the bridge over the Miljacka and get to Grandma and Grandad. He came running back, all upset, sweating with fear and sadness. They're all right, thank God. Tito Street looks awful. The heavy shelling has destroyed shop windows, cars, flats, the fronts and roofs of buildings. Luckily, not too many people were hurt because they managed to take shelter. Neda (Mummy's girlfriend) rushed over to see how we were and to tell us that they were OK and hadn't had any damage. But it was terrible.

We talked through the window with Auntie Boda and Bojana just now. They were in the street yesterday when that heavy shooting broke out. They managed to get to Stela's cellar.

Zlata

A Bosnian woman collects her belongings after her house was destroyed by bombing.

Tuesday, 5 May 1992

Dear Mimmy,

The shooting seems to be dying down. I guess they've
caused enough misery, although I don't know why. It
has something to do with politics. I just hope the
'kids' [a popular term for politicians] come to some
agreement. Oh, if only they would, so we could live
and breathe as human beings again. The things that
have happened here these past few days are terrible.
I want it to stop for ever. PEACE! PEACE!
    I didn't tell you, Mimmy, that we've rearranged
things in the flat. My room and Mummy's and Daddy's
are too dangerous to be in. They face the hills,
which is where they're shooting from. If only you
knew how scared I am to go near the windows and into
those rooms. So, we turned a safe corner of the
sitting room into a 'bedroom'. We sleep on mattresses
on the floor. It's strange and awful. But, it's safer
that way. We've turned everything around for safety.
We put Cicko in the kitchen. He's safe there,
although once the shooting starts there's nowhere
safe except the cellar. I suppose all this will stop
and we'll go back to our usual places.

    Ciao!
        Zlata

Sunday, 17 May 1992

Dear Mimmy,

It's now definite: there's no more school. The war
has interrupted our lessons, closed down the
schools, sent children to cellars instead of
classrooms. They'll give us the grades we got at the
end of last term. So I'll get a report card saying
I've finished fifth grade.

Ciao!
Zlata

During the war, there was often no running water in
Sarajevo. When there was no shooting, Zlata would help her
parents to collect water in bottles.

Wednesday, 20 May 1992

Dear Mimmy,

The shooting has died down. Today Mummy felt
brave enough to cross the bridge. She saw
Grandma and Grandad, ran into various people
she knows and heard a lot of sad news. She came
back all miserable. Her brother was wounded on
14 May, driving home from work. Her brother is
hurt and she doesn't find out about it until
today — that's terrible. He was wounded in the
leg and is in hospital. How can she get to him?
It's like being at the other end of the world
now. They told her he's all right, but she
doesn't believe them and keeps crying. If only
the shooting would stop, she could go to the
hospital. She says: 'I won't believe it until I
see him with my own eyes.'

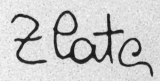

Monday, 25 May 1992

Dear Mimmy,

Today the Zetra Hall, the Olympic Zetra, went up in
flames. The whole world knew about it, it was the Olympic
beauty, and now it's going up in flames. The fire-fighters
tried to save it, and our Žika joined them. But it didn't
stand a chance. The forces of war don't know anything
about love and the
desire to save
something. They just
know how to destroy,
burn, take things away.
So they wanted Zetra to
disappear as well. It
makes me sad, Mimmy.
  I feel as though no
one and nothing here
will survive.

Your

Zlata

The biggest building
in Sarajevo burned
down after a night of
heavy shelling.

Wednesday, 27 May 1992

Dear Mimmy,

SLAUGHTER! MASSACRE! HORROR! CRIME! BLOOD! SCREAMS! TEARS! DESPAIR!

That's what Vaso Miskin Street looks like today. Two shells exploded in the street and one in the market. Mummy was near by at the time. She ran to Grandma's and Grandad's. Daddy and I were beside ourselves because she hadn't come home. I saw some of it on TV and I still can't believe what I actually saw. It's unbelievable. I've got a lump in my throat and a knot in my tummy. HORRIBLE. They're taking the wounded to the hospital. It's a madhouse. We kept going to the window hoping to see Mummy, but she wasn't back. They released a list of the dead and wounded. Daddy and I were tearing our hair out. We didn't know what had happened to her. Was she alive? At 16.00, Daddy decided to go and check the hospital. He got dressed, and I got ready to go to the Bobars', so as not to stay at home alone. I looked out the window one more time and ... I SAW MUMMY RUNNING ACROSS THE BRIDGE. As she came into the house she started shaking and crying. Through her tears she told us how she had seen dismembered bodies. All the neighbours came because they had been afraid for her. Thank God, Mummy is with us. Thank God.

A HORRIBLE DAY. UNFORGETTABLE. HORRIBLE! HORRIBLE!

Your

Zlata

Saturday, 30 May 1992

Dear Mimmy,

The City Maternity Hospital has burned down. I was born there. Hundreds of thousands of new babies, new residents of Sarajevo, won't have the luck to be born in this maternity hospital now. It was new. The fire devoured everything. The mothers and babies were saved. When the fire broke out two women were giving birth. The babies are alive. God, people get killed here, they die here, they disappear, things go up in flames here, and out of the flames, new lives are born.

Your

Zlata

Finally, when she arrived in Paris, Zlata could have a normal childhood again.

Afterword

Zlata continued to write her diary throughout 1992 and 1993. She recorded the worsening conditions brought about by the war and how the family coped without running water, gas or electricity. She also wrote about the results of the direct hits from Serbian shelling and of the individual deaths of family friends. In February 1993, Zlata wrote 'God, I keep thinking this is going to stop. But the war just goes on and on.'

But for Zlata, her diary proved to be her passport to freedom. On December 23 1993, after a French company published the diary, Zlata and her parents were taken to Paris with the help of the French government and UNPROFOR (United Nations Protection Force).

Soon after, Zlata's diary was translated into over 30 languages. Interviewed in Paris, Zlata spoke of her feelings about leaving Sarajevo: 'I feel guilty that if I want a Coke, I can have it. I can go to the Disney store round the corner and look at all the toys and games, but then I think of my little friend back home, who is four. She has no toys and has never known anything but war.'

As the siege went on, it claimed more that 10,500 lives, with thousands more being wounded. The fighting eventually stopped in February 1994 when the countries of NATO (North Atlantic Treaty Organization) intervened to bring about a cease-fire. The Serbian forces withdrew their tanks and under a peace plan in 1995, the city stayed united.

Life is finally being restored to war-torn Sarajevo.

Brian Moses

Right: Yugoslavia's position in Europe.

Below: A map of Yugoslavia as it was in 1991/92, before the war.

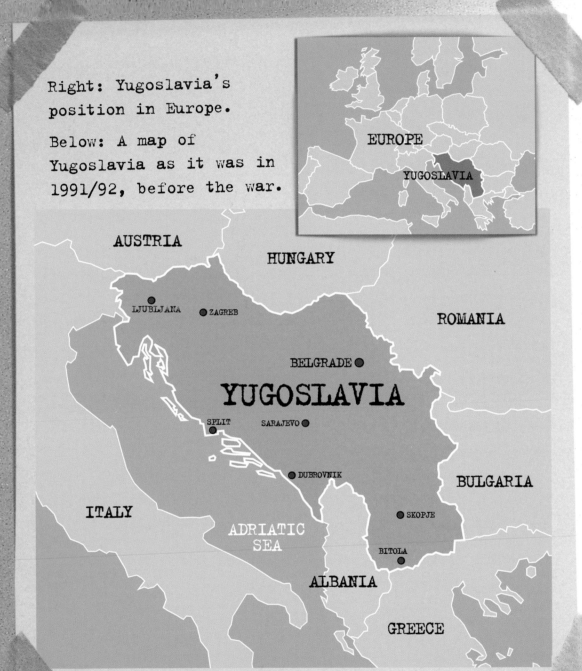

EUROPE

YUGOSLAVIA

AUSTRIA

HUNGARY

ROMANIA

LJUBLJANA

ZAGREB

BELGRADE

YUGOSLAVIA

SPLIT

SARAJEVO

DUBROVNIK

BULGARIA

ITALY

ADRIATIC SEA

SKOPJE

BITOLA

ALBANIA

GREECE

Below: Yugoslavia became SIX new
countries - Slovenia, Croatia, Serbia,
Montenegro, Macedonia and Bosnia-
Herzegovina, where Zlata's family lived.

Index